A CHRISTMAS CAROL:
30 KEY QUOTATIONS
FOR GCSE

ANTHONY MARKHAM

ANGRY SWAN PRESS

Contents

"Marley was dead: to begin with."

The opening line of Charles Dickens' novella "A Christmas Carol" is one of the most iconic and memorable in all of literature: "Marley was dead: to begin with." This seemingly simple statement holds profound significance, serving as the cornerstone upon which the entire story is built. Let's delve into the various layers of meaning and symbolism inherent in this line.

1. Introduction of Marley's Death: The line is straightforward in its announcement that Jacob Marley, a key character in the story, is no longer alive. This is a dramatic and attention-grabbing way to commence the narrative. The unequivocal declaration of Marley's death immediately establishes the story's central premise and prepares the reader for the supernatural elements that will soon unfold.

2. Setting the Tone: The fact that the novella begins with death immediately sets a sombre and somewhat eerie tone. The idea of death and the afterlife is a recurring theme throughout the story, making it an appropriate starting point.

3. A Symbol of Change: The mention of Marley's death serves as a symbol of transformation. It highlights the idea that death is not just a physical end but a metaphorical one as well. Scrooge's transformation from a cold, selfish, and miserly old man into a compassionate and generous figure is central to the story, and Marley's death foreshadows the potential for transformation in Scrooge himself.

4. Marley's Role as a Catalyst: Marley's death is not merely an event in the past; it's the catalyst for the events of the story. His visitation as a ghost to Scrooge on Christmas

Eve is what propels the entire narrative. Marley serves as a cautionary figure, warning Scrooge of the consequences of his own greed and selfishness.

5. Reflection on Life and Regret: The opening line indirectly invites the reader to contemplate the nature of life and the inevitability of death. Marley's death underscores the regret that many people feel when they reach the end of their lives and realize they've squandered opportunities for kindness and connection.

6. The Supernatural Element: The novella is a ghost story, and by opening with Marley's death, Dickens immediately introduces the supernatural aspect of the tale. This line sets the stage for the arrival of Marley's ghost and, eventually, the three spirits who will visit Scrooge to teach him important life lessons.

In essence, the opening line, "Marley was dead: to begin with," is a masterful stroke of storytelling. It not only conveys essential information but also establishes the tone, theme, and underlying philosophy of the entire narrative. It prompts readers to reflect on life, death, and the potential for transformation, making it a fitting beginning to a timeless and enduring classic.

"There is a man and a boy here."

The line "There is a man and a boy here" appears in the opening stave of Charles Dickens' novella, "A Christmas Carol." It's part of a dialogue between Scrooge, the story's protagonist, and two charity workers who have come to his office on Christmas Eve to seek donations for the poor. While seemingly straightforward, this line encapsulates several layers of meaning and significance, revealing key aspects of Scrooge's character, the society in which he lives, and the thematic core of the novella.

1. Scrooge's Character: This line immediately introduces us to Ebenezer Scrooge, the central character, and reveals his miserly and callous nature. Scrooge's response to the charity workers is cold and dismissive, as he refers to them simply as "a man and a boy." His failure to address them by their names or show any interest in their cause underscores his lack of compassion and empathy. This sets the stage for his transformation throughout the story.

2. The Generosity Gap: The line underscores the stark contrast between Scrooge and the charity workers. While they are there to raise funds to alleviate the suffering of the poor during the Christmas season, Scrooge embodies the complete opposite attitude, caring only about his own wealth and showing no concern for the well-being of others. The "man and a boy" represent the selflessness and generosity that Scrooge lacks.

3. Social Commentary: Dickens uses this interaction to comment on the social disparities and indifference of the wealthy towards the poor in Victorian society. The charity workers are symbolic of those who strive to make a positive impact, whereas

Scrooge represents the upper class that often turned a blind eye to the suffering of the less fortunate.

4. Foreboding of Future Encounters: This line foreshadows Scrooge's encounters with the three Christmas spirits who will visit him later in the story. The "man and a boy" can be seen as precursors to these supernatural beings, as they are the first to challenge Scrooge's worldview and confront him with the consequences of his actions.

5. A Path to Redemption: The presence of the charity workers, as revealed by this line, also provides an early opportunity for Scrooge to begin his journey of redemption. The question becomes whether he will embrace this opportunity or continue down his selfish and cold-hearted path.

6. The Spirit of Christmas: In a broader context, this line embodies the spirit of Christmas itself. Christmas is traditionally a time of giving, love, and charity. The "man and a boy" embody this spirit by seeking help for the less fortunate, while Scrooge, at this point in the story, represents the antithesis of that spirit.

"There is a man and a boy here" serves as a pivotal moment in "A Christmas Carol." It introduces us to the central conflict of the story, highlighting Scrooge's character flaws and the social issues of the time. It also sets the stage for the transformative journey that Scrooge is about to undertake, from a heartless miser to a benevolent and compassionate individual, in the true spirit of Christmas.

QUOTATION 3

"I wear the chain I forged in life."

The line "I wear the chain I forged in life" is a powerful and pivotal statement made by Jacob Marley's ghost in Charles Dickens' novella, "A Christmas Carol." This quote is central to the story's themes of redemption, the consequences of one's actions, and the potential for change. Let's delve into the depth and significance of this statement.

1. Marley's Revelation: In "A Christmas Carol," Jacob Marley is the former business partner of Ebenezer Scrooge, and he appears as a ghost to warn Scrooge of the consequences of his life choices. Marley's ghost is laden with heavy chains, locks, ledgers, and cash boxes. When he utters this line, he is explaining to Scrooge the reason for his ghostly appearance and the burden he now carries in the afterlife. Marley's words reveal that the chains he bears were created during his lifetime, representing his own moral and ethical failings.

2. Symbol of Regret and Redemption: Marley's chains are symbolic of the mistakes and misdeeds he committed during his earthly existence. They are not physical chains but metaphysical ones forged through his greed and selfishness. Marley is not merely a ghost but a tormented soul seeking redemption. His message to Scrooge serves as a warning that the choices one makes in life have a profound impact on one's eternal fate.

3. Consequences of Greed and Selfishness: Marley's chains, laden with ledgers and cash boxes, symbolize the weight of his own avarice and disregard for others. The line underscores the idea that one's actions have lasting consequences, both in this life and the afterlife. It's a stark reminder of the moral responsibility each individual holds for

their own choices and their impact on society.

4. Scrooge's Wake-Up Call: Marley's statement serves as a pivotal moment in the story. It shocks Scrooge and sets the stage for the visits from the three Christmas spirits who will guide him through a transformative journey. Scrooge, initially dismissive of Marley's ghost, begins to comprehend the severity of his own chain in the making and the potential for his redemption.

5. A Universal Lesson: Marley's proclamation extends beyond the story's context and serves as a universal lesson for readers. It prompts reflection on the personal chains that individuals might be forging through their actions, whether positive or negative. The line encourages us to consider the legacies we are creating and how our choices impact our own lives and the lives of others.

6. Redemption and Change: Ultimately, Marley's message is not just about condemnation but about the possibility of redemption. His haunting serves as an opportunity for Scrooge to alter the course of his own life and escape a similar fate. This message of hope and transformation is at the heart of the novella's theme, emphasizing that it's never too late to change and to live a life of compassion and generosity.

"I wear the chain I forged in life" is a profound and thought-provoking line in "A Christmas Carol." It is a reminder of the enduring consequences of one's actions, the potential for redemption, and the universal theme of personal responsibility. This line contributes significantly to the novella's enduring relevance and its status as a timeless classic that continues to inspire reflection and positive change.

"Mankind was my business."

The statement "Mankind was my business" is a pivotal and poignant line spoken by Jacob Marley's ghost in Charles Dickens' classic novella, "A Christmas Carol." This line embodies the core theme of the story and carries a profound message about the importance of compassion, responsibility, and the interconnectedness of humanity. Let's explore the depth and significance of this statement:

1. A Declaration of Regret and Redemption: Marley's ghost utters this line to Ebenezer Scrooge when asked about the purpose of his visit. It's an admission of his own shortcomings in life, particularly his indifference to the suffering of others. Marley expresses regret for not having fulfilled his duty to humanity and his obligation to help those in need. This line establishes Marley's desire for redemption, both in his own afterlife and by warning Scrooge not to follow the same path.

2. A Fundamental Theme of the Story: The line "Mankind was my business" is central to the novella's core message. Dickens uses Marley's character as a vehicle to highlight the contrast between self-serving, greedy behavior and selflessness and compassion. Marley's posthumous realization serves as a cautionary tale, reminding the reader of the importance of caring for the welfare of others.

3. Social Critique: Dickens uses the character of Marley to critique the societal ills of his time. The Victorian era was marked by stark class divisions and economic inequality, and Dickens was a vocal advocate for social reform. Through Marley, he highlights the moral responsibility of the privileged to address these injustices and assist those less fortunate.

4. The Chains of Selfishness: Marley's chains, laden with cash-boxes, ledgers, and heavy purses, symbolize the encumbrance of his own selfishness and greed. The statement "Mankind was my business" conveys that Marley's ultimate responsibility was not merely to accumulate wealth but to make a positive impact on the lives of others. His chains are a metaphor for the burdens carried by those who prioritize material gain over the welfare of their fellow human beings.

5. A Call to Action: Beyond Marley's personal confession, this line challenges Scrooge, and by extension, the reader, to reconsider their own priorities and actions. It urges us to recognize our shared humanity and the moral obligation to contribute to the betterment of society. Marley's ghost, though deceased, conveys a sense of urgency in addressing these matters.

6. The Power of Transformation: Marley's statement encapsulates the central message of "A Christmas Carol" – that it is never too late to change one's ways and that personal transformation is possible. Marley's purpose is to offer Scrooge a chance for redemption and to inspire him to embrace the spirit of Christmas by showing kindness and generosity to others.

"Mankind was my business" is a profound and compelling line in "A Christmas Carol." It encapsulates the essence of the story's moral message, highlighting the responsibilities we bear toward our fellow human beings. It encourages readers to reflect on their own actions and priorities, fostering a sense of empathy, responsibility, and the transformative power of compassion. Dickens masterfully uses Marley's confession to emphasize the enduring relevance of these themes and their capacity to inspire positive change in individuals and society as a whole.

QUOTATION 5

"Bah! Humbug!"

The exclamation "Bah! Humbug!" is one of the most iconic and memorable lines in Charles Dickens' novella, "A Christmas Carol." Uttered by the story's central character, Ebenezer Scrooge, it encapsulates his disdain for the Christmas season and everything it represents. This line has become synonymous with Scrooge's character and the idea of cynicism and negativity during the holidays. Let's explore the depth and significance of this phrase:

1. Scrooge's Characterization: "Bah! Humbug!" is introduced early in the story when Scrooge is approached by his nephew, Fred, who wishes him a Merry Christmas. Scrooge's response instantly characterizes him as a gruff, miserly, and uncharitable individual. His dismissal of the holiday spirit reveals his isolation and detachment from the warmth and goodwill associated with Christmas.

2. Rejection of Tradition: Scrooge's use of the phrase reflects his rejection of traditional holiday customs. He sees Christmas traditions like gift-giving, feasting, and carol-singing as frivolous and wasteful. His "Humbug" dismisses these traditions as empty and insincere, representing a rejection of sentimental customs in favor of practicality and financial gain.

3. Symbol of Cynicism: "Bah! Humbug!" is a quintessential expression of cynicism. It embodies a negative and skeptical outlook on the world. Scrooge's view of Christmas as a humbug suggests that he believes it to be a deceptive, fraudulent, and hollow celebration. He perceives the goodwill and generosity of the season as a sham.

4. Isolation and Loneliness: Scrooge's refusal to engage with the holiday spirit highlights his self-imposed isolation. He pushes away friends, family, and the community, leading to a life of loneliness and bitterness. His use of "Bah! Humbug!" symbolizes his emotional detachment from the people around him.

5. Greed and Materialism: Scrooge's obsession with wealth and money is also evident in this phrase. By declaring "Humbug," he emphasizes his belief in the supremacy of materialism over sentiment. He sees the commercialization of Christmas as a pointless exercise and a distraction from his primary focus on financial profit.

6. Transformation and Redemption: The evolution of this phrase is central to the novella's message. As the story progresses and Scrooge is visited by the three spirits, his attitude toward Christmas and life undergoes a profound transformation. By the end of the story, he has renounced "Bah! Humbug!" and wholeheartedly embraced the spirit of the season, demonstrating the potential for personal growth and redemption.

7. Universal Theme* "Bah! Humbug!" transcends the context of the novella and becomes a symbol of the general resistance people often exhibit toward positive change, compassion, and empathy. It encourages readers to reflect on their own cynicism, barriers to happiness, and resistance to the joy and goodwill that can be found in the world.

"Bah! Humbug!" is a succinct and powerful expression that encapsulates Ebenezer Scrooge's character and the themes of cynicism, materialism, and transformation found in "A Christmas Carol." The phrase serves as a touchstone for the novella's message of personal growth, redemption, and the enduring capacity of individuals to embrace the warmth of the holiday season and, by extension, the warmth of human connection and kindness.

QUOTATION 6

"I am the Ghost of Christmas Past."

The line "I am the Ghost of Christmas Past" is a significant declaration in Charles Dickens' novella, "A Christmas Carol." It is made by one of the three spirits who visit Ebenezer Scrooge on Christmas Eve, taking him on a transformative journey through his own past. This line represents a pivotal moment in the story, encapsulating the spirit's identity and purpose, as well as conveying several deeper themes:

1. Introduction of the Supernatural Element: The line "I am the Ghost of Christmas Past" marks the first appearance of the supernatural in the story. It sets the stage for the otherworldly, mystical journey that Scrooge is about to embark upon. The spirit's declaration immediately captures the reader's attention and creates a sense of anticipation.

2. Nostalgia and Memory: The spirit's identity is rooted in the concept of memory and nostalgia. It is a representation of Scrooge's own past, particularly his past Christmases. This ties into the broader theme of the role that memories and experiences play in shaping an individual's character and choices.

3. The Power of Reflection: The spirit of Christmas Past serves as a powerful symbol of the value of reflecting on one's life. By taking Scrooge back in time, the spirit provides an opportunity for self-examination and understanding. It underscores the importance of examining one's past actions and the impact they have had on one's character and relationships.

4. Repentance and Change: The spirit's purpose is not to merely revisit the past

11

but to facilitate Scrooge's transformation. It shows Scrooge both the moments of joy and the moments of sorrow in his past, with the goal of prompting remorse for his mistakes and inspiring a desire to change. The spirit's role aligns with the overall theme of redemption and personal growth.

5. The Ghost as a Guide: Throughout the novella, the spirits serve as guides and educators, helping Scrooge gain insights into his own life. In the case of the Ghost of Christmas Past, this role is particularly pronounced. The spirit guides Scrooge through various scenes, encouraging him to observe, reflect, and learn from his past.

6. Childhood Innocence and Lost Joy: The spirit's presence also allows the reader to explore Scrooge's past, particularly his childhood and youth. These glimpses reveal a younger Scrooge who was more innocent, joyful, and full of potential. The contrast between his past self and his present demeanour underscores the idea that people often lose some of their childlike joy and optimism as they grow older and become consumed by the demands of adulthood.

7. The Multilayered Nature of Time: The phrase "I am the Ghost of Christmas Past" underscores the idea that time is a complex and multi-layered concept. The past is not a monolithic, unchanging entity but a dynamic force that continues to influence the present and future. It highlights how one's past experiences continue to shape their identity and choices.

"I am the Ghost of Christmas Past" in "A Christmas Carol" signifies the introduction of the supernatural and the beginning of Scrooge's transformative journey. It emphasizes the importance of memory, reflection, and the potential for change. The spirit's role as a guide and educator aligns with the novella's themes of redemption and personal growth while also highlighting the multifaceted nature of time and the enduring influence of one's past.

"A solitary child, neglected by his friends."

The phrase "A solitary child, neglected by his friends" is a poignant and evocative description found in Charles Dickens'' novella, "A Christmas Carol." This statement, uttered by the Ghost of Christmas Past as he shows Ebenezer Scrooge scenes from his own past, carries a deep and resonant significance within the story. Let's explore the layers of meaning and themes encapsulated by this phrase:

1. Childhood Isolation: The phrase captures a moment from Scrooge's past, revealing him as a lonely and isolated child. It evokes a sense of solitude and neglect that is deeply rooted in his early years. This portrayal underscores the idea that Scrooge's transformation into a miserly and cold-hearted adult is, in part, a response to his experiences as a child.

2. The Consequences of Neglect: The description "neglected by his friends" draws attention to the consequences of isolation and neglect during one's formative years. It suggests that Scrooge's early experiences contributed to the development of his distant and unfeeling adult persona. Neglect can lead to a sense of emotional distance and a lack of empathy.

3. The Lost Joy of Childhood: The image of a solitary and neglected child serves as a powerful contrast to Scrooge's adult self. It hints at a time when Scrooge may have experienced the innocence, wonder, and joy of childhood but was subsequently deprived of those emotions by the circumstances of his upbringing. It reminds readers of the potential for happiness that is often lost in adulthood.

4. The Power of Memories: This phrase is a reminder of the potency of memories. The Ghost of Christmas Past uses Scrooge's own memories to prompt him to reevaluate his life choices and actions. It underscores the idea that personal growth and transformation can be achieved through the recollection and analysis of one's own past.

5. Themes of Regret and Redemption: Scrooge's lonely childhood and his sense of being neglected underscore the broader themes of regret and redemption in "A Christmas Carol." The story invites readers to reflect on the choices they've made in life and the potential for redemption, even when one has followed a path of selfishness and isolation.

6. Human Connection and Compassion: The solitary and neglected child in this phrase also highlights the importance of human connection and compassion. It serves as a reminder that, through understanding and kindness, people can alleviate the suffering of others, particularly those who may be experiencing loneliness and neglect.

7. A Call to Empathy: "A solitary child, neglected by his friends" serves as a call to empathy and understanding. It encourages the reader to consider the impact of their actions on others, particularly on those who may be vulnerable or isolated.

A solitary child, neglected by his friends" in "A Christmas Carol" is a poignant representation of Scrooge's past and a poignant reminder of the power of memories, the consequences of neglect, and the potential for personal transformation. It is a pivotal moment in the story, illustrating how Dickens uses the past to encourage reflection and change in the present and future.

"I wish... to see my tenderness, connected with a Christmas day."

The statement "I wish... to see my tenderness, connected with a Christmas day" is a profound and emotionally charged moment in Charles Dickens' novella, "A Christmas Carol." It is spoken by Ebenezer Scrooge when he is visited by the Ghost of Christmas Past, who has taken him on a journey through his own memories. This phrase encapsulates a pivotal theme in the story and reveals the depth of Scrooge's character. Let's explore the layers of meaning and significance embedded in this line:

1. Yearning for Connection: The phrase "I wish" signifies a deep yearning within Scrooge's heart. It reveals a longing for a sense of connection, warmth, and love that he has long suppressed. Scrooge's desire to see his tenderness suggests that he once possessed the capacity for empathy, compassion, and love, but it has become dormant over the years.

2. Tenderness and Regret: Scrooge's wish reflects his regret for having strayed from the path of tenderness and compassion. The phrase highlights the regret he feels for having neglected his own emotional well-being and the well-being of others. It's a poignant moment of self-reflection and an admission of his own shortcomings.

3. Nostalgia and Sentimentality: The phrase is deeply rooted in nostalgia and sentimentality, particularly in the context of Christmas. Christmas is traditionally a time for warmth, love, and the rekindling of human connections. Scrooge's yearning to connect tenderness with Christmas suggests that he longs for the warmth and joy

that the holiday symbolizes.

4. The Ghost's Role as a Catalyst: The Ghost of Christmas Past acts as a catalyst for Scrooge's transformation. It prompts him to confront his own emotions and the choices he has made in life. By taking Scrooge on a journey through his past, the spirit awakens dormant feelings and memories that have been buried deep within Scrooge's heart.

5. The Possibility of Redemption: This phrase underscores one of the central themes of "A Christmas Carol": the potential for personal redemption. It implies that it is never too late to rediscover one's capacity for tenderness, empathy, and love. Scrooge's wish for tenderness connected to Christmas suggests that he is open to the possibility of change.

6. The Healing Power of Christmas: Scrooge's wish highlights the healing and transformative power of Christmas. The holiday season has the ability to bring out the best in people, to foster compassion, and to rekindle relationships. It is a time when individuals are encouraged to look beyond themselves and extend goodwill to others.

7. Reconnecting with Humanity: The phrase "I wish" is an expression of Scrooge's desire to reconnect with his own humanity and with the broader human community. It signifies his recognition of the importance of empathy and love in fostering deeper connections with others.

"I wish... to see my tenderness, connected with a Christmas day" is a moment of emotional revelation and longing in "A Christmas Carol." It represents the potential for transformation and personal redemption, as well as the healing power of Christmas. Scrooge's wish conveys the universal message that it is never too late to rediscover tenderness and empathy and to embrace the warmth and love of the holiday season.

QUOTATION 9

"These are but shadows of the things that have been."

The line "These are but shadows of the things that have been" is spoken by the Ghost of Christmas Past in Charles Dickens' "A Christmas Carol." It is a significant and thought-provoking statement that carries profound implications regarding the nature of memory, the passage of time, and the relationship between the past, the present, and the future. Let's explore the depth and significance of this phrase:

1. The Power of Memory: The statement underscores the idea that our memories are imperfect and often incomplete. What we remember of our past is merely a shadow or an approximation of the actual events and experiences. It acknowledges the fallibility of human memory and how our recollections can be influenced by emotions, biases, and the passage of time.

2. The Role of Nostalgia: "These are but shadows" highlights the role of nostalgia in shaping our perceptions of the past. Nostalgia can cast a rosy glow on our memories, emphasizing the positive aspects and downplaying the negatives. The phrase suggests that the past may not be as idyllic as we remember it, and the "shadows" can obscure the complexity of past experiences.

3. The Influence of the Past on the Present: The Ghost of Christmas Past's role is to show Scrooge the memories and experiences that have shaped him. This statement serves as a reminder that our past experiences, whether accurately remembered or not, have a profound influence on who we are in the present. Scrooge's journey through

17

his past serves as an opportunity for him to reflect on the origins of his own character and behaviour.

4. The Elusiveness of Time: The phrase "shadows of the things that have been" alludes to the elusive and fleeting nature of time. It suggests that the past is not a fixed, concrete entity but something that is constantly shifting and evolving in our minds. The past is as changeable as the present and the future.

5. The Regret and Nostalgia Duality: "These are but shadows" captures the duality of regret and nostalgia. While some memories may evoke nostalgia and warmth, others may bring regret and sorrow. This duality underscores the importance of learning from our past, making amends when necessary, and striving for personal growth and redemption.

6. The Theme of Change: The phrase aligns with the novella's central theme of personal transformation and redemption. It prompts Scrooge to confront his past, acknowledge his own flaws and mistakes, and consider the potential for change. It underscores the idea that individuals have the power to shape their future by learning from their past.

7. The Philosophical Aspect: Philosophically, the line "These are but shadows" invites reflection on the nature of reality and perception. It resonates with the idea that our experience of the world is mediated by our senses and consciousness, and what we perceive as reality is, to some extent, a construct of our minds.

"These are but shadows of the things that have been" is a profound and multifaceted statement in "A Christmas Carol." It delves into the complexities of memory, the impact of the past on the present, and the potential for personal growth and transformation. It underscores the idea that the past is not fixed but continually evolving in our minds, and it encourages us to consider the lessons and insights it can offer for our lives.

"There was a boy singing a Christmas carol at my door."

The statement "There was a boy singing a Christmas carol at my door" is a vivid and evocative scene from Charles Dickens' novella, "A Christmas Carol." It is part of a memory that the Ghost of Christmas Past shares with Ebenezer Scrooge as they journey through Scrooge's own past. This scene represents a pivotal moment in the story and encapsulates several essential themes and ideas:

1. The Power of Christmas Music: The image of a boy singing a Christmas carol at the door is a vivid portrayal of the role of music in evoking the spirit of the holiday season. Christmas carols have a unique ability to inspire warmth, joy, and a sense of community. The boy's song serves as a catalyst for the emotions and memories associated with Christmas.

2. The Role of Children: The presence of a young boy is a reminder of the innocence and hope that children embody. In many ways, children serve as the embodiment of the Christmas spirit with their unbridled enthusiasm and sense of wonder. The boy's singing represents the purity and simplicity of the holiday's joys.

3. The Contrast with Scrooge's Current Self: The memory of the boy singing a Christmas carol sharply contrasts with the present-day Scrooge. At the time of this memory, Scrooge may have been more open to the joys of Christmas. The contrast underscores the stark change that has occurred in Scrooge's life, and it prompts him to reflect on the reasons for his transformation into a bitter, miserly old man.

4. The Theme of Redemption**: This memory is a pivotal point in Scrooge's transformation. It stirs deep emotions and serves as a turning point in the story. It is an opportunity for Scrooge to confront his past and reconnect with the warmth and goodwill of Christmas. The memory ultimately contributes to his desire for redemption and change.

5. **Community and Connection: The presence of the boy singing a Christmas carol also highlights the idea of community and connection. Christmas is a time when people come together to celebrate, share, and support one another. The boy's singing represents the communal aspect of the holiday, underscoring the importance of shared traditions and the bonds of friendship and family.

6. The Role of the Past: This memory, like others experienced during Scrooge's journey with the Ghost of Christmas Past, emphasizes the impact of past experiences on one's present character and behavior. It illustrates how a single event or memory can shape an individual's outlook and choices.

7. The Revival of Emotion: The image of the boy singing reawakens emotions and memories that Scrooge has long suppressed. It reminds him of the capacity for joy, compassion, and connection that he once possessed. This revival of emotion is crucial in prompting his transformation.

In summary, the scene "There was a boy singing a Christmas carol at my door" is a significant and emotionally charged moment in "A Christmas Carol." It captures the power of Christmas music, the contrast between Scrooge's past and present, and the theme of redemption and personal growth. This memory serves as a catalyst for Scrooge's transformation, prompting him to reevaluate his choices and embrace the warmth and goodwill of the holiday season.

QUOTATION 11

"I am the Ghost of Christmas Present."

The statement "I am the Ghost of Christmas Present" is a crucial declaration in Charles Dickens' novella, "A Christmas Carol." It marks the arrival of the second of the three spirits that visit Ebenezer Scrooge on Christmas Eve, each with the goal of facilitating his transformation and redemption. This line encapsulates the spirit's identity and its significance in the story, as well as conveying broader themes and messages:

1. Spirit of the Moment: The Ghost of Christmas Present represents the spirit of the current Christmas season. It embodies the idea that the present moment, with its festivities, celebrations, and human connections, is a time of immense importance. This spirit emphasizes the value of living in the present, cherishing the "now," and finding joy in the company of loved ones.

2. Joy and Abundance: The Ghost of Christmas Present is often depicted as a jolly, larger-than-life figure. It symbolizes the joy, abundance, and generosity associated with the Christmas season. This spirit is surrounded by a cornucopia of food, drink, and holiday delicacies, underlining the themes of plenty and goodwill.

3. Family and Community: The spirit's portrayal highlights the significance of family and community during the holidays. It is often shown interacting with a wide range of people, emphasizing the importance of human connection and the warmth of shared experiences. This spirit's presence underscores the idea that Christmas is a time to come together and celebrate with loved ones.

4. Empathy and Compassion: The Ghost of Christmas Present serves as a symbol of empathy and compassion. It inspires Scrooge to look beyond his own self-interest and to consider the welfare of others, particularly the Cratchit family and Tiny Tim. This spirit's role is pivotal in fostering Scrooge's empathy and encouraging him to contribute positively to the lives of those in need.

5. The Theme of Transformation: The arrival of the Ghost of Christmas Present signals a turning point in Scrooge's journey of transformation. Scrooge is moved by the warmth, generosity, and happiness that surround the spirit, and this experience profoundly impacts his outlook on life and the holiday season.

6. The Concept of Time: The phrase "I am the Ghost of Christmas Present" underscores the concept of time and the notion that the present moment is fleeting and should be cherished. This spirit highlights the ephemeral nature of the holidays and encourages individuals to make the most of the time they have with loved ones.

7. The Possibility of Change: The Ghost of Christmas Present embodies the idea that change is possible. It prompts Scrooge to recognize the opportunities for personal growth and the potential to reshape his future through acts of kindness, generosity, and goodwill.

In conclusion, "I am the Ghost of Christmas Present" represents the embodiment of the current holiday season's spirit and the themes of joy, abundance, family, community, and transformation. This spirit's presence in "A Christmas Carol" serves as a catalyst for Scrooge's journey toward redemption and reinforces the enduring message that Christmas is a time for empathy, compassion, and the celebration of the present moment.

"There is never enough time to do or say all the things that we would wish."

The statement "There is never enough time to do or say all the things that we would wish" is a poignant and universal reflection on the nature of time, human relationships, and the unfulfilled desires that many people carry throughout their lives. This sentiment is found in "A Christmas Carol" when the Ghost of Christmas Present is showing Ebenezer Scrooge scenes of the holiday season. Let's explore the profound implications and themes associated with this statement:

1. Temporal Limitations: This statement acknowledges the finite nature of time. It conveys the idea that human existence is bound by temporal constraints, and as a result, individuals often find themselves unable to accomplish all they desire in their lifetimes. This recognition of life's brevity serves as a reminder to use time wisely and make the most of the present.

2. Unfulfilled Wishes: The phrase "all the things that we would wish" touches on the concept of unfulfilled desires and aspirations. It acknowledges that there are dreams, goals, and expressions of love or gratitude that remain unspoken or unachieved due to the constraints of time. This notion invites reflection on the importance of prioritizing meaningful actions and expressions of affection.

3. The Value of Communication: The statement highlights the significance of communication and expressing one's feelings to others. In many cases, regrets arise from not having said "I love you," "I'm sorry," or "Thank you" often enough. It

emphasizes the importance of fostering open and honest relationships while time allows.

4. Regret and Redemption: The sentiment "never enough time" evokes a sense of regret. In the context of "A Christmas Carol," Scrooge is shown these scenes to confront his own regrets and the opportunities for redemption and personal transformation. This theme encourages readers to consider their own regrets and the potential for positive change.

5. The Power of Prioritization: The statement encourages individuals to reflect on their priorities and make choices that align with their deepest wishes and values. It prompts the question of whether one's time is spent on what truly matters, be it in terms of family, relationships, or personal pursuits.

6. The Ephemeral Nature of Life: It underscores the transient nature of life itself. The reality of human mortality is an inescapable fact, and this statement serves as a reminder that our lives are finite. It encourages individuals to make the most of the time they have, both in terms of personal growth and in nurturing relationships.

7. The Need for Mindfulness: In the rush and busyness of daily life, people often forget to express their love, gratitude, or affection. This sentiment calls for mindfulness, urging individuals to be more present and aware of the opportunities to convey their feelings to others.

"There is never enough time to do or say all the things that we would wish" is a reflective and contemplative statement that carries a powerful message about the limitations of time, the importance of relationships and communication, the role of regret, and the potential for positive change. It underscores the idea that life's brevity should inspire individuals to prioritize what truly matters and to cherish the moments they have with loved ones.

QUOTATION 13

"This boy is Ignorance. This girl is Want."

The line "This boy is Ignorance. This girl is Want." is a stark and symbolic moment in Charles Dickens' novella, "A Christmas Carol." It is a declaration made by the Ghost of Christmas Present as he reveals two wretched and emaciated children concealed beneath his robe. This statement serves as a powerful metaphor for societal issues and carries several layers of meaning:

1. Social Commentary: Dickens used his works to critique the social and economic disparities of his time, particularly the suffering of the poor and the indifference of the wealthy. "This boy is Ignorance. This girl is Want" encapsulates his social commentary by vividly illustrating the consequences of poverty, ignorance, and neglect.

2. Ignorance: The boy, representing Ignorance, symbolizes the lack of education and knowledge that perpetuated the cycle of poverty and suffering among the lower classes. Dickens believed that the ignorance of the poor, particularly children, was a grave injustice, as it denied them opportunities for advancement.

3. Want: The girl, representing Want, symbolizes the material deprivation and poverty that many individuals endured during the Victorian era. She embodies the physical and emotional suffering experienced by those who lacked the basic necessities of life, including food, shelter, and warmth.

4. Interconnected Issues: The pairing of Ignorance and Want emphasizes the interconnectedness of these issues. Ignorance can perpetuate poverty, and poverty can limit access to education and knowledge. Dickens highlights how these problems

rce each other and create a cycle of despair.

5. Responsibility and Moral Obligation: By presenting Ignorance and Want in this dramatic and poignant manner, Dickens conveys a moral message. He challenges readers, and particularly those in positions of privilege and power, to recognize their moral obligation to address the suffering of the less fortunate and to work toward social change and reform.

6. The Duality of Christmas: The appearance of Ignorance and Want during the Christmas season emphasizes the duality of the holiday. While Christmas is often associated with joy, generosity, and abundance, it is also a time when the suffering of the less fortunate is acutely felt. The presence of these children reminds us of the importance of extending help and compassion during the holiday season.

7. Scrooge's Redemption: This moment in the story plays a crucial role in Scrooge's transformation. It serves as a catalyst for his personal awakening and commitment to change. Witnessing Ignorance and Want stirs deep emotions in Scrooge, prompting him to pledge his assistance to those in need and to prioritize their well-being.

In conclusion, "This boy is Ignorance. This girl is Want" is a striking and evocative metaphor that captures the social issues of Dickens' time and carries enduring relevance. It serves as a powerful call to action, urging society to address the intertwined problems of ignorance and poverty, to recognize the moral responsibility toward the less fortunate, and to prioritise compassion and social reform, particularly during the holiday season.

"If they would rather die, they had better do it, and decrease the surplus population."

The statement "If they would rather die, they had better do it, and decrease the surplus population" is a callous and morally reprehensible viewpoint expressed by Ebenezer Scrooge in Charles Dickens' "A Christmas Carol." It represents one of the most striking and memorable instances of Scrooge's extreme miserliness and disregard for the well-being of others. This statement encapsulates several critical themes and social issues:

1. Misanthropy and Selfishness: Scrooge's statement reflects his deep-seated misanthropy and extreme selfishness. He views people in poverty as burdens on society and shows a complete lack of empathy for their suffering. His perspective is grounded in a callous individualism that prioritizes personal wealth and dismisses social responsibility.

2. Social Inequality: The phrase highlights the stark social inequalities of the Victorian era in which the story is set. Scrooge's sentiment is indicative of a broader societal attitude that marginalized and devalued the poor, treating them as expendable members of society.

3. Dehumanization: Scrooge's words dehumanize the impoverished by reducing them to numbers in an economic equation. By referring to them as "surplus population," he strips them of their humanity, compassionately dismissing their suffering as insignificant and dispensable.

Critique of Capitalism: Dickens used "A Christmas Carol" as a vehicle for critiquing the negative consequences of unrestrained capitalism and the pursuit of profit at the expense of social welfare. Scrooge's heartless stance is an embodiment of the callousness often associated with unchecked capitalism.

5. The Impact of Individual Choices: Scrooge's statement underscores the power of individual choices in perpetuating or ameliorating societal problems. His attitude reflects the idea that personal choices and attitudes, especially among those in positions of power and privilege, have a profound impact on the well-being of society as a whole.

6. The Possibility of Redemption: Scrooge's transformation throughout the story serves as a central theme. His initial callousness and later redemption highlight the potential for personal growth and a shift from selfishness to compassion. This transformation represents a hopeful message of change and the possibility of redemption for even the most hardened individuals.

7. Social Responsibility: The phrase stands in stark contrast to the spirit of Christmas and the message of goodwill and charity that is central to the holiday. It serves as a reminder of the importance of social responsibility and the duty to care for the less fortunate.

In conclusion, the statement "If they would rather die, they had better do it, and decrease the surplus population" is a stark and chilling portrayal of Ebenezer Scrooge's extreme miserliness and indifference to the suffering of the poor. It reflects broader issues of social inequality, dehumanization, and the consequences of unchecked capitalism. However, the story ultimately offers hope through Scrooge's transformation, emphasizing the potential for redemption and the importance of social responsibility and compassion.

QUOTATION 15

"God bless us, every one!"

The exclamation "God bless us, every one!" is one of the most iconic lines from Charles Dickens' "A Christmas Carol." It is spoken by the character Tiny Tim, the youngest son of Bob Cratchit, Scrooge's underpaid and impoverished clerk. This simple but powerful phrase encapsulates several profound themes and emotions central to the novella:

1. Hope and Optimism: When Tiny Tim utters this phrase, it is a poignant expression of hope and optimism, particularly in the face of adversity. Despite his own serious illness and his family's dire financial situation, Tiny Tim's heartfelt wish for blessings upon everyone reflects an unwavering belief in the possibility of goodness and generosity in the world.

2. The Spirit of Christmas: "God bless us, every one!" captures the true spirit of Christmas. It is a reminder that Christmas is a time for unity, compassion, and the spreading of goodwill to all, regardless of social status or economic circumstances. The phrase reinforces the idea that Christmas is about extending kindness and blessings to one's fellow human beings.

3. Contrast with Scrooge's Transformation: The line is particularly significant in contrast to Scrooge's earlier attitude of indifference and callousness. Scrooge's transformation is driven, in part, by his witnessing the genuine warmth and love in the Cratchit family. The innocence and optimism of Tiny Tim directly influence Scrooge's change of heart.

ulnerable and Disadvantaged: Tiny Tim's proclamation shines a spotlight plight of the vulnerable and disadvantaged members of society, especially en. His fragile health and the Cratchit family's financial struggles serve as a inder of the hardships faced by many during Dickens' time.

5. Emphasis on Blessings Over Material Wealth: The phrase underscores the idea that true blessings extend beyond material wealth. It emphasizes the importance of emotional and spiritual riches, such as love, family, and compassion. It conveys the message that these intangible blessings are often the most valuable.

6. The Power of a Single Phrase: Despite its brevity, "God bless us, every one!" carries profound meaning. It highlights the impact that simple expressions of kindness and good wishes can have on individuals and their communities. A single phrase can carry the spirit of Christmas and encourage others to embrace its principles.

7. Unity and Inclusivity: The line promotes a sense of unity and inclusivity, emphasizing that blessings should be extended to all, without exception. It encourages the idea that, during the holiday season and beyond, people should strive for harmony and togetherness.

"God bless us, every one!" represents the heart of "A Christmas Carol" and the essence of the holiday season. It conveys hope, optimism, and the true spirit of Christmas, emphasizing the value of blessings that go beyond material wealth. The line serves as a powerful reminder of the importance of compassion, unity, and extending goodwill to all, particularly to those who are vulnerable or disadvantaged.

"I am in the presence of the Ghost of Christmas Yet To Come."

The statement "I am in the presence of the Ghost of Christmas Yet To Come" marks a pivotal and eerie moment in Charles Dickens' "A Christmas Carol." It signifies the arrival of the third and final spirit that visits Ebenezer Scrooge on Christmas Eve. The Ghost of Christmas Yet To Come, also known as the Ghost of Christmas Future, is a foreboding and enigmatic figure, representing the unknown and the consequences of one's actions. This statement carries several significant themes and emotions:

1. Foreboding and Fear: The arrival of the Ghost of Christmas Yet To Come is filled with foreboding and fear. Its dark and silent demeanour, draped in a shroud, conveys a sense of impending doom and mystery. This spirit represents the uncertainty of the future and the potential consequences of one's choices.

2. The Nature of Time: The phrase emphasizes the inexorable passage of time. The Ghost of Christmas Yet To Come symbolizes the inexorable march of time, the inevitability of change, and the unknown nature of the future. It underscores the importance of making wise choices in the present because they shape what lies ahead.

3. The Impact of One's Actions* This statement serves as a reminder that the consequences of one's actions are not limited to the present but extend into the future. Scrooge is confronted with a vision of the future that highlights the results of his past choices, particularly his selfishness and lack of compassion.

4. The Power of Redemption: The presence of the Ghost of Christmas Yet To Come is a critical part of Scrooge's journey of transformation. It prompts him to confront the potential bleakness of his own future and serves as a catalyst for him to seek redemption and change. It illustrates that it is never too late to alter one's path and make amends.

5. Facing the Unknown: The statement reflects the universal fear of the unknown. The future is inherently uncertain, and people often fear what lies ahead. Scrooge's encounter with this spirit symbolizes the human desire to understand, control, and prepare for what is yet to come.

6. Mortality and the Afterlife: The presence of the Ghost of Christmas Yet To Come also touches on themes of mortality and the afterlife. In Dickens' Victorian context, death was a topic often avoided, and the spirit represents the inevitability of death and the mysteries of what follows.

7. Reflection and Self-Examination: The arrival of this spirit encourages self-reflection and introspection. Scrooge is confronted with the consequences of his actions and is prompted to examine the choices he has made. It challenges him to consider how he wants to be remembered and what legacy he wishes to leave.

In conclusion, the statement "I am in the presence of the Ghost of Christmas Yet To Come" is a critical moment in "A Christmas Carol." It embodies themes of time, consequences, redemption, and the fear of the unknown future. The spirit's appearance prompts Scrooge to confront his past and consider the possibility of a brighter, more compassionate future, illustrating the power of transformation and the importance of making choices that shape one's destiny.

"I am not the man I was."

The statement "I am not the man I was" is a pivotal moment in Charles Dickens' "A Christmas Carol." It is spoken by Ebenezer Scrooge during his transformation and redemption after his encounters with the three Christmas spirits. This phrase encapsulates the central theme of personal growth and serves as a profound reflection on the capacity for change and self-improvement. Here's an exploration of the various facets of this statement:

1. Acknowledgment of Change: The phrase "I am not the man I was" signifies Scrooge's realization that he has undergone a fundamental transformation. He acknowledges that he has evolved as a person, not just in terms of his behaviour but also in his beliefs, attitudes, and values.

2. The Power of Self-Reflection: Scrooge's transformation is driven by a process of self reflection prompted by the visitations of the Christmas spirits. This phrase underscores the idea that self-examination and introspection can lead to personal growth and the reevaluation of one's choices and character.

3. Redemption and Reformation: Scrooge's acknowledgement of change represents the theme of redemption in "A Christmas Carol." It shows that, even for individuals who have led a life of greed and selfishness, there is the potential for reformation, atonement, and the pursuit of a more virtuous and compassionate path.

4. The Influence of Experience: Scrooge's encounters with the Christmas spirits and the visions of his past, present, and future have a profound impact on his

perception of himself and the world. These experiences force him to reevaluate his past actions and make the decision to change.

5. Inspiration for Others: Scrooge's transformation serves as an inspirational example for others. His acknowledgement of change demonstrates that people can evolve and improve throughout their lives, and his story encourages empathy and compassion in others.

6. The Message of Hope: The phrase "I am not the man I was" carries a message of hope, suggesting that personal growth and transformation are possible at any stage in life. It conveys the idea that one's past actions and mistakes need not define their future.

7. A Break from the Past: The statement marks a break from Scrooge's previous identity as a miserly, callous individual. It symbolises the shedding of his old self and the emergence of a new, kinder, and more generous persona.

8. The Ripple Effect: Scrooge's transformation has a positive ripple effect on his relationships and community. His acknowledgement of change contributes to the well-being and happiness of those around him, particularly the Cratchit family and Tiny Tim.

In summary, "I am not the man I was" is a powerful declaration of personal growth and transformation in "A Christmas Carol." It embodies the themes of redemption, self-reflection, and the potential for positive change. Scrooge's journey from miser to benefactor serves as a timeless example of the capacity for individuals to evolve, make amends, and create a brighter future for themselves and those they touch.

"Before I draw nearer to that stone to which you point, answer me one question."

The statement "Before I draw nearer to that stone to which you point, answer me one question" is a moment of significance in Charles Dickens' "A Christmas Carol." It is spoken by Ebenezer Scrooge during his encounter with the Ghost of Christmas Yet To Come, or the Ghost of Christmas Future. This phrase marks a pivotal point in the story and carries several layers of meaning:

1. Desire for Knowledge: Scrooge's request for an answer before approaching the grave underscores his desire for knowledge and understanding. He is eager to comprehend the significance of the scene unfolding before him, especially the identity of the person whose death is being discussed.

2. Fear of the Unknown: Scrooge's question also reflects his fear of the unknown. The ghostly figure is shrouded in mystery, and the scene at the gravesite is foreboding. Scrooge's question serves as an expression of his anxiety about what the future holds and his need for reassurance.

3. The Power of Information: Scrooge recognizes the power of information and its ability to shape his perspective. He understands that having his question answered will provide context and understanding, allowing him to make sense of the events he is witnessing.

4. The Importance of Communication: The phrase highlights the significance

of clear communication and the exchange of information. Scrooge's request for an answer reflects the idea that open and honest communication is crucial in any situation, including when confronting fear or uncertainty.

5. Reconciliation with the Future: Scrooge's request indicates his willingness to reconcile with the future, even though it appears bleak. By asking a question and seeking understanding, he demonstrates his readiness to confront the consequences of his past actions and to take responsibility for his own future.

6. The Role of Curiosity: Scrooge's question embodies the role of curiosity and the pursuit of knowledge as catalysts for personal growth. His curiosity prompts him to engage with the ghost and the visions of the future, leading to his ultimate transformation.

7. A Moment of Vulnerability: Scrooge's question also signifies a moment of vulnerability. He is no longer the obstinate, unyielding miser he once was. He is willing to admit his lack of knowledge and seek answers, indicating a significant shift in his character.

In conclusion, the phrase "Before I draw nearer to that stone to which you point, answer me one question" is a moment of emotional depth and transformation in "A Christmas Carol." It underscores the themes of fear, curiosity, the pursuit of knowledge, and the willingness to engage with the unknown. Scrooge's request for an answer demonstrates his readiness to reconcile with his past, face the consequences of his actions, and embrace the potential for a brighter future.

"I see a vacant seat."

The statement "I see a vacant seat" is a powerful moment in Charles Dickens' "A Christmas Carol." It is spoken by the character Ebenezer Scrooge during his visit with the Ghost of Christmas Present as they look upon the Cratchit family's Christmas dinner. This simple observation carries profound meaning and represents several themes and emotions:

1. Symbol of Loss: When Scrooge utters, "I see a vacant seat," he is drawing attention to the empty chair at the Cratchit family's Christmas table. This vacant seat represents the loss of Tiny Tim, who is not present at the festive gathering. This observation serves as a poignant reminder of the vulnerability of human life, particularly in the face of illness and poverty.

2. Empathy and Compassion: Scrooge's comment highlights his evolving empathy and compassion. He is no longer the heartless and miserly character he once was. His observation of the vacant seat reflects his deepening connection with the Cratchit family and his genuine concern for Tiny Tim's well-being.

3. Theme of Redemption: The sight of the vacant seat plays a crucial role in Scrooge's journey of redemption. It elicits profound emotions in him and serves as a catalyst for his commitment to change. It prompts him to inquire about Tiny Tim's fate and seek a better outcome for the Cratchit family.

4. **The Fragility of Life**: The vacant seat also underscores the fragility of life, particularly in the context of the 19th century when access to healthcare was limited.

It reminds readers of the harsh living conditions that many faced and the impact on the most vulnerable, such as children.

5. Social Injustice: The sight of the empty chair is a symbol of the social injustice and economic inequality of the time. It highlights the struggles faced by the Cratchit family and the need for compassion and assistance for those less fortunate.

6. The Joy of Togetherness: Scrooge's observation of the vacant seat serves as a contrast to the joy and togetherness of the Christmas dinner. It emphasizes the importance of family, community, and shared moments during the holiday season.

7. The Possibility of Change: The statement also symbolizes the potential for change and the power of individual actions. Scrooge's transformation from a miserly, indifferent character to a caring and compassionate one illustrates the capacity for personal growth and the ability to make a positive impact on the lives of others.

"I see a vacant seat" is a profound moment in "A Christmas Carol." It symbolizes themes of loss, empathy, redemption, the fragility of life, social injustice, the joy of togetherness, and the potential for personal change. Scrooge's observation of the vacant seat serves as a turning point in the story and underscores the importance of compassion and community during the holiday season.

QUOTATION 20

"The bed was his own, the room was his own."

The statement "The bed was his own, the room was his own" is a transforming moment in Charles Dickens' "A Christmas Carol." It is a reflection of Ebenezer Scrooge's realization and transformation at the end of the novella, following his encounters with the three Christmas spirits. This phrase symbolizes several key themes and emotions:

1. Ownership and Reclamation: "The bed was his own, the room was his own" signifies the reclamation of Scrooge's personal space. Earlier in the story, Scrooge's living quarters are depicted as bleak and unwelcoming, mirroring his cold and isolated existence. This moment represents his reacquisition of not just material possessions but also his own life and identity.

2. Redemption and Second Chances: The statement captures the theme of redemption and the idea that it's never too late for a second chance. Scrooge has transformed from a miserly, selfish, and isolated individual to one who values his connections with others and actively seeks to make amends.

3. The Power of Transformation: "The bed was his own, the room was his own" underscores the power of personal transformation. Scrooge's journey from darkness to enlightenment is a testament to the human capacity for change, growth, and self-improvement.

4. Comfort and Warmth: The description of the bed and room being "his own" represents not just physical comfort but also emotional warmth. Scrooge has not only gained back his material possessions but has found a sense of belonging and contentment.

5. The Importance of Home: The statement emphasizes the significance of the concept of "home." Scrooge's room and bed are more than physical spaces; they represent a sense of safety, familiarity, and the emotional centre of one's life.

6. Reconnection with Humanity: Scrooge's reclaimed bed and room signify his reconnection with humanity. He has transitioned from being a person who viewed others with indifference and disdain to one who values relationships, community, and the joy of shared experiences.

7. A Return to Tradition: The phrase also highlights the return to traditional values and the spirit of Christmas. Scrooge's room, once cold and barren, now symbolizes the warmth, generosity, and goodwill associated with the holiday.

8. Joy and Celebration: The line encapsulates the joy and celebration that come with personal transformation. It is a culmination of Scrooge's newfound understanding of the holiday season and his embrace of the spirit of Christmas.

In summary, "The bed was his own, the room was his own" is a powerful moment in "A Christmas Carol." It signifies themes of ownership, redemption, personal transformation, the comfort of home, the importance of connections, and the joy of the holiday season. Scrooge's reclamation of his room and bed represents a renewed sense of self and a return to the values of love, compassion, and the celebration of life.

QUOTATION 21

"I am as light as a feather, I am as happy as an angel, I am as merry as a schoolboy."

The exclamation "I am as light as a feather, I am as happy as an angel, I am as merry as a schoolboy" is a moment of profound joy and elation in Charles Dickens' "A Christmas Carol." It is spoken by Ebenezer Scrooge during his transformation, specifically when he awakens on Christmas morning after his encounters with the three Christmas spirits. This statement conveys a range of emotions and themes:

1. Rebirth and Renewal: The exclamation embodies the theme of rebirth and renewal. Scrooge's description of feeling "as light as a feather" suggests the shedding of his heavy, burdensome past, including his selfishness and indifference. He is reborn as a compassionate, joyful person.

2. Emotional Liberation: The phrase represents emotional liberation. For years, Scrooge had been weighed down by his miserly and unkind ways. Now, he is free from the emotional chains that had bound him. The lightness he feels symbolizes the release from his previous emotional constraints.

3. The Spirit of Christmas: The exclamation captures the essence of the Christmas spirit. Scrooge's newfound happiness, joy, and light-heartedness align with the core values of Christmas, which emphasize goodwill, generosity, and the celebration of life.

4. Inner Child and Innocence: The comparison to being "as merry as a schoolboy" reflects the recapturing of Scrooge's inner child and innocence. He rediscovers the

unadulterated joy of youth, emphasizing the idea that the spirit of
[...] s can rekindle the childlike wonder in all of us.

[...] 5. Atonement and Redemption: Scrooge's elation also signifies his redemption and atonement. His previous actions and attitudes had distanced him from others and from the joy of life. This exclamation is a symbol of his desire to make amends and reintegrate with society.

6. Change and Transformation: The phrase represents the profound change and transformation that can occur in a person. Scrooge's character has undergone a remarkable evolution, illustrating the potential for growth, empathy, and positive change in individuals.

7. Positive Outlook: The statement reflects a shift in Scrooge's outlook on life. He has gone from viewing the world through a lens of pessimism and cynicism to one of optimism and hope. He now sees the beauty and goodness in the world around him.

8. Embracing Life: Scrooge's words express an embrace of life and a readiness to experience its fullness. He is no longer preoccupied with material wealth but is focused on the richness of human connections, joy, and the happiness of the present moment.

In summary, the exclamation "I am as light as a feather, I am as happy as an angel, I am as merry as a schoolboy" marks a transformative moment in "A Christmas Carol." It signifies themes of rebirth, emotional liberation, the spirit of Christmas, inner child-like wonder, atonement, change, a positive outlook, and the embrace of life. Scrooge's elation is not just a personal transformation but also an invitation for readers to embrace the holiday spirit and the potential for joy and growth in their own lives.

QUOTATION 22

"Scrooge was better than his word."

The phrase "Scrooge was better than his word" is a redeeming moment in Charles Dickens' "A Christmas Carol." It appears toward the end of the novella when Ebenezer Scrooge, having undergone a profound transformation, is reflecting on the changes he has made in his life. This statement encapsulates several important themes and emotions:

1. Redemption and Transformation: "Scrooge was better than his word" signifies Scrooge's redemption and transformation as a character. Throughout the story, Scrooge evolves from a miserly and unfeeling individual into someone who is generous, compassionate, and empathetic. He has not only promised to change but has taken concrete actions to improve himself and the lives of those around him.

2. The Power of Personal Growth: This phrase underscores the remarkable power of personal growth and the human capacity for change. It serves as a reminder that, no matter how entrenched in one's ways or how many mistakes have been made, it is never too late to become a better person and to make amends.

3. The Importance of Actions: Scrooge's actions speak louder than his words. While he initially makes a commitment to the spirits and to himself to change, the true measure of his transformation is in the kindness and generosity he demonstrates in his interactions with others. His actions are a testament to his sincerity.

4. **Repairing Relationships**: "Scrooge was better than his word" signifies the repair of damaged relationships. Throughout the story, Scrooge reconciles with his

nephew, Fred, and with his employee, Bob Cratchit. He not only mends these relationships but also strengthens them through his newfound warmth and kindness.

5. The Ripple Effect of Kindness: Scrooge's transformation and improved character have a positive ripple effect on those around him. The phrase highlights the impact of his actions on the Cratchit family, Tiny Tim, and others in his community. It emphasizes the idea that small acts of kindness can create significant positive changes.

6. The Contrast with His Former Self: The statement contrasts Scrooge's current behaviour with his former miserly nature. It emphasizes the drastic change he has undergone, showcasing the stark difference between the old Scrooge and the new, reformed Scrooge.

7. A Message of Hope: "Scrooge was better than his word" conveys a message of hope and optimism. It inspires readers to believe in the possibility of change, to recognize the importance of one's actions, and to embrace the potential for a brighter future.

In summary, "Scrooge was better than his word" is a moment of personal redemption and transformation in "A Christmas Carol." It symbolises themes of growth, the power of actions, the repair of relationships, the ripple effect of kindness, and the potential for a hopeful and optimistic future. It serves as a testament to the capacity of individuals to change for the better and make a positive impact on the lives of others.

"I will honour Christmas in my heart and try to keep it all the year."

The statement "I will honour Christmas in my heart and try to keep it all the year" is a profound and pivotal moment in Charles Dickens' "A Christmas Carol." It is spoken by Ebenezer Scrooge during the culmination of his transformation when he awakens on Christmas morning with a renewed spirit and a commitment to embrace the values of Christmas throughout the entire year. This statement embodies several significant themes and emotions:

1. Embracing the Spirit of Christmas: Scrooge's pledge to honour Christmas reflects his newfound understanding of the holiday's true meaning. Throughout the story, he transitions from viewing Christmas as a time of inconvenience and expense to recognizing it as a time of love, compassion, and goodwill. His declaration is a promise to carry the essence of Christmas with him always rather than confining it to a single day.

2. A Commitment to Change: The phrase signifies Scrooge's profound transformation as a character. He has transitioned from a miserly, self-centred individual to someone who is committed to being a better, more generous, and more compassionate person. It represents his acknowledgement that true change is not temporary but should be a continuous effort.

3. The Power of Redemption: Scrooge's commitment to keep Christmas in his heart year-round serves as a symbol of redemption and atonement. He recognizes his

past shortcomings and is determined to make amends and live a life characterized by kindness and generosity.

4. The Influence of Experience: This declaration underscores the transformative influence of Scrooge's experiences with the three Christmas spirits. These encounters have prompted him to reevaluate his life, recognize the impact of his actions, and strive for personal growth and improvement.

5. A Message of Universal Goodwill* The statement conveys the universal message of goodwill and compassion that is central to the holiday season. It encourages the idea that the values of love, kindness, and generosity should not be limited to a specific time but should be embraced and practised consistently.

6. Reconnection with Humanity: Scrooge's commitment symbolizes his reconnection with humanity and his desire to be an active and compassionate member of society. He has transitioned from a solitary existence to one where he actively engages with and cares for others.

7. A Call to Readers: The phrase also serves as a call to readers, encouraging them to embrace the holiday spirit and its values in their own lives. It challenges individuals to extend acts of kindness and goodwill year-round and to make a positive difference in their communities.

"I will honour Christmas in my heart and try to keep it all the year" is a moment of profound transformation and commitment in "A Christmas Carol." It signifies the central themes of embracing the spirit of Christmas, continuous personal growth, redemption, universal goodwill, reconnection with humanity, and the call for readers to carry the values of the holiday with them throughout the year. Scrooge's pledge serves as a timeless reminder of the importance of kindness, compassion, and generosity in our daily lives.

"It's a wonderful pudding!"

The exclamation "It's a wonderful pudding!" is a delightful moment in Charles Dickens' "A Christmas Carol." It is spoken by Bob Cratchit, Scrooge's underpaid and humble clerk, during the Cratchit family's Christmas dinner. This seemingly simple statement carries several layers of meaning and significance:

1. Appreciation of Simple Pleasures: Bob Cratchit's enthusiastic comment about the pudding reflects a core theme of the novella - the appreciation of life's simple and joyful moments. Despite the Cratchit family's financial struggles, they find happiness in the little things, such as sharing a special meal together on Christmas Day.

2. Resilience and Optimism: Bob Cratchit's remark also underscores the Cratchit family's resilience and optimism in the face of adversity. They choose to focus on the positive aspects of their lives, like their love for each other, rather than dwelling on their lack of material wealth.

3. Christmas Spirit: The enthusiasm over the pudding embodies the true spirit of Christmas as depicted in the novella. It is a time of celebration, togetherness, and joy, where people come together to share in the simple pleasures of life.

4. Contrast with Scrooge: Bob Cratchit's excitement over the pudding is in stark contrast to Scrooge's earlier attitude of miserliness and indifference. Scrooge's transformation is driven, in part, by witnessing the genuine warmth and happiness in the Cratchit family. The pudding serves as a symbol of the joy and generosity that Scrooge has been missing in his life.

5. Symbol of Generosity: The pudding also symbolizes the Cratchit family's generosity. Despite their limited resources, they are willing to share their special treat with Scrooge, emphasizing the value of giving and sharing during the holiday season.

6. Unity and Family: The pudding represents the unity and family bonds that are central to the holiday season. Christmas is a time when families come together to celebrate and strengthen their connections, and the enjoyment of a festive meal is a key element of this tradition.

7. Optimism for the Future: Bob Cratchit's enthusiastic comment implies a sense of hope and optimism for the future. The joy and gratitude the Cratchit family finds in their modest celebration suggest that, no matter the hardships they face, they have faith in better times to come.

In summary, the exclamation "It's a wonderful pudding!" represents the heartwarming and optimistic spirit of the Cratchit family in "A Christmas Carol." It signifies the appreciation of life's simple pleasures, resilience, the true Christmas spirit, the contrast with Scrooge's former attitude, the generosity of sharing, family unity, and a hopeful outlook. This moment in the story reminds readers of the importance of finding joy in the little things and the power of love and togetherness during the holiday season.

"It's easy to feel a little forlorn, forlorn."

The statement "It's easy to feel a little forlorn, forlorn" encapsulates a sense of sadness and melancholy, emphasizing the depths of loneliness or despair that a person can experience. This phrase can be viewed from several angles, each of which provides insight into its meaning and emotional significance:

1. Repetition for Emphasis: The repetition of the word "forlorn" in the statement amplifies the emotion and underscores the depth of the feeling. It suggests that the emotional state is not just a passing mood but a profound sense of desolation.

2. The Human Experience: The phrase captures a universal aspect of the human experience. At various points in life, everyone encounters moments of sadness or loneliness, where they may indeed feel "forlorn." The emotional state described is relatable and part of the human condition.

3. Seasonal Blues: In the context of "A Christmas Carol," this statement may also allude to the idea that, despite the festive holiday season, some individuals may experience a sense of loneliness or sadness. It highlights the contrast between the joyful spirit of Christmas and the emotions that many people may still grapple with during this time.

4. Scrooge's Transformation: The phrase can be connected to Ebenezer Scrooge's character development in the novella. Before his transformation, Scrooge is depicted as a forlorn and isolated individual, consumed by his greed and indifference to others. However, the story shows that even the most forlorn of individuals can find

redemption and positive change in their lives.

5. A Call for Empathy: The phrase may serve as a call for empathy and compassion. It encourages readers to recognize and reach out to those who may be feeling forlorn or lonely during the holiday season or at any time. It underscores the importance of extending a hand of friendship and support to those in need.

6. The Complexity of Emotions: The use of the word "easy" in the statement also suggests the complexity of human emotions. It can be easy to slip into a state of sadness or melancholy, but it can also be challenging to climb out of it. This complexity of emotions is a recurring theme in Dickens' works.

In conclusion, the phrase "It's easy to feel a little forlorn, forlorn" conveys a sense of deep sadness and loneliness, which is a common human experience. It has emotional depth and serves as a reminder of the importance of understanding and supporting those who may be going through difficult times. In "A Christmas Carol," it resonates with the broader theme of transformation and the potential for individuals to move from a forlorn state to one of greater hope and connection.

"I will honour Christmas in my heart and try to keep it all the year."

This quote, spoken by Scrooge, reflects the central theme of the story: the transformation of a man who learns to embrace the spirit of Christmas and carry it with him throughout the entire year. It emphasizes the importance of kindness, generosity, and goodwill in one's life. The statement "I will honour Christmas in my heart and try to keep it all the year" is a profound and pivotal moment in Charles Dickens' "A Christmas Carol." It is spoken by Ebenezer Scrooge during his transformation, following his encounters with the three Christmas spirits. This declaration represents a rich tapestry of themes and emotions:

1. Embracing the True Spirit of Christmas: Scrooge's commitment to "honour Christmas in my heart" signifies his newfound understanding of the holiday's genuine meaning. It encapsulates his transition from viewing Christmas as a time of inconvenience and expense to recognizing it as a time of love, compassion, and goodwill. He pledges to carry the essence of Christmas with him year-round rather than limiting it to a specific day.

2. A Commitment to Change: This phrase serves as a symbol of Scrooge's profound transformation as a character. He evolves from a miserly, self-centred individual into someone determined to be a better, more generous, and more compassionate person. It represents his acknowledgement that authentic change is not a temporary fix but should be a constant effort.

3. The Power of Redemption: Scrooge's commitment also symbolizes his redemption and atonement. He recognizes his past wrongdoings and is resolute in his desire to make amends and lead a life characterized by kindness and generosity.

4. The Influence of Experience: This declaration underscores the transformative influence of Scrooge's experiences with the three Christmas spirits. These encounters prompt him to reevaluate his life, acknowledge the consequences of his actions, and strive for personal growth and self-improvement.

5. A Message of Universal Goodwill: The statement conveys the universal message of goodwill and compassion that is central to the holiday season. It encourages the idea that the values of love, kindness, and generosity should not be restricted to a specific time but should be embraced and practised consistently.

6. Reconnection with Humanity: Scrooge's commitment symbolizes his reconnection with humanity and his determination to be an active and compassionate member of society. He shifts from a solitary existence to one where he actively engages with and cares for others.

7. A Call to Readers: The phrase also serves as a call to readers, encouraging them to embrace the holiday spirit and its values in their own lives. It challenges individuals to extend acts of kindness and goodwill year-round and to make a positive difference in their communities.

In summary, "I will honour Christmas in my heart and try to keep it all the year" is a moment of profound transformation and commitment in "A Christmas Carol." It signifies the central themes of embracing the spirit of Christmas, continuous personal growth, redemption, universal goodwill, reconnection with humanity, and the call for readers to carry the values of the holiday with them throughout the year. Scrooge's pledge serves as a timeless reminder of the importance of kindness, compassion, and generosity in our daily lives.

QUOTATION 27

"They sought the pawnbroker's shops to buy golden wonders."

The quote "They sought the pawnbroker's shops to buy golden wonders" from "A Christmas Carol" by Charles Dickens is a reflection of the commercialization of Christmas and the extent to which people have focused on materialism rather than the true spirit of the holiday. This statement speaks to several important aspects of the story and carries a deeper message:

1. Materialism and the Holiday Season: The mention of people seeking pawnbroker's shops for "golden wonders" highlights the way in which the holiday season has become associated with excessive consumerism. People are driven to purchase expensive gifts and ornaments, often straining their financial resources in the pursuit of what they believe will bring joy and fulfilment.

2. Emphasis on Wealth and Possessions: The term "golden wonders" suggests that these items are not just ordinary gifts but opulent and valuable objects. This speaks to the societal emphasis on wealth and material possessions, which can lead to shallow and unfulfilling experiences during the holiday season.

3. The Distracting Nature of Materialism: In the context of the story, the pursuit of material possessions and "golden wonders" serves as a distraction from the true spirit of Christmas. Instead of focusing on love, generosity, and spending time with loved ones, people are fixated on the acquisition of wealth and status symbols.

4. Scrooge's Transformation: The quote is particularly significant in light of Scrooge's transformation. His own obsession with wealth and financial success is the antithesis of the Christmas spirit. As the story progresses, he undergoes a profound change, recognizing that the pursuit of "golden wonders" is shallow and unfulfilling. He comes to understand that genuine happiness and meaning in life are found in relationships, compassion, and kindness.

5. A Critique of Society: Through this quote, Dickens critiques the values and priorities of society during the Victorian era and, by extension, raises questions about the contemporary consumer-driven culture. It prompts readers to reflect on the extent to which materialism has overshadowed the true essence of the holiday season.

In summary, the quote "They sought the pawnbroker's shops to buy golden wonders" in "A Christmas Carol" serves as a commentary on the commercialization of Christmas, the distraction of materialism from the holiday's true spirit, and the transformative journey that characters like Scrooge undertake to reevaluate their priorities and rediscover the importance of human connection and compassion during the holiday season.

"Scrooge could not feel it himself, but this was clearly the case; for though the Ghost sat perfectly motionless, its hair, and skirts, and tassels, were still agitated as by the hot vapour from an oven."

The quote "Scrooge could not feel it himself, but this was clearly the case; for though the Ghost sat perfectly motionless, its hair, and skirts, and tassels, were still agitated as by the hot vapour from an oven" is a poignant and significant moment in "A Christmas Carol" that underscores the transformational journey of Ebenezer Scrooge. This quote provides several layers of meaning and serves as a turning point in the story:

1. The Ghost's Emotional Energy: The passage describes the Ghost of Christmas Present, who exudes warmth, kindness, and joy. Even though Scrooge, in his initial state of cynicism and indifference, cannot personally feel or perceive these emotions, the physical manifestations of the Ghost's vitality are unmistakable. The agitated hair, skirts, and tassels represent the vibrant and energetic spirit of Christmas that is being offered to Scrooge.

2. The Contrast with Scrooge's State of Mind: Scrooge's heart has been frozen by a lifetime of greed and selfishness. At this point in the story, he is still struggling to fully embrace the holiday spirit. The fact that he "could not feel it himself" underscores the

depth of his transformation that still needs to occur. The Ghost's radiant presence serves as a sharp contrast to Scrooge's cold and lifeless existence.

3. A Symbol of Transformation: The agitated appearance of the Ghost's attire can be seen as a visual representation of the transformative power of the Christmas spirit. It suggests that the holiday has the capacity to thaw even the coldest of hearts and to invigorate individuals with the warmth of compassion, love, and human connection.

4. Foreshadowing Scrooge's Change: The quote serves as a foreshadowing of Scrooge's eventual change of heart. Although he may not fully grasp the significance of this experience at this moment, it marks the beginning of his awakening to the true meaning of Christmas. As the story unfolds, he begins to absorb and reflect the warmth and goodwill radiating from the Ghost and the holiday season.

5. The Universality of the Christmas Spirit: The quote reflects the idea that the spirit of Christmas is not confined to one's personal feelings or beliefs but is a universal force that has the potential to touch all individuals, even those who may initially resist its influence.

In summary, the quote "Scrooge could not feel it himself, but this was clearly the case; for though the Ghost sat perfectly motionless, its hair, and skirts, and tassels, were still agitated as by the hot vapour from an oven" is a pivotal moment in "A Christmas Carol." It conveys the transformative power of the Christmas spirit, the stark contrast between Scrooge's initial state of indifference and the warmth of the Ghost, and the potential for even the most hardened individuals to experience a change of heart and embrace the true spirit of the holiday.

"My time grows short."

Spoken by the Ghost of Christmas Present, this quote reminds Scrooge of the limited time for positive change and the importance of embracing the present moment. The quote "My time grows short" is spoken by the Ghost of Christmas Present in Charles Dickens' "A Christmas Carol." It marks a significant moment in the story and carries a profound message. Here, we'll explore the various dimensions and implications of this statement:

1. Temporal Urgency: The Ghost's declaration that "My time grows short" conveys a sense of urgency and the ephemeral nature of his existence. It reminds Scrooge that the spirit's time in the present is limited, and they must make the most of the time they have. This temporal constraint adds tension to the narrative, as it suggests that there is much to learn and experience in a limited span.

2. Emphasis on the Present: The Ghost of Christmas Present embodies the spirit of the current moment. This declaration encourages Scrooge to live in the present and fully embrace the joys and opportunities of the here and now. It underscores the idea that the present is a gift, and one should not squander it by dwelling on the past or worrying about the future.

3. The Fleeting Nature of Time: The phrase "My time grows short" is a reminder of the fleeting nature of time itself. It suggests that time marches on, whether we are ready or not, and serves as a reflection on the inevitability of change. It encourages readers and Scrooge to make the most of the time they have and to appreciate life's precious moments.

Lesson in the Transience of Life:** This statement can be seen as a broader
on. In the context of the story, it highlights the importance of living a life of
ness, generosity, and connection while we have the opportunity, for life is fleeting.
urges individuals to value the time they have with loved ones and to make positive
ontributions to society.

5. Foreshadowing the Ghost's Departure: The Ghost's acknowledgement that his time is running out foreshadows his imminent departure and the arrival of the next spirit, the Ghost of Christmas Yet To Come. This transition signals a change in the narrative, as Scrooge will be led to confront his own future.

6. Personal Transformation: The statement also contributes to Scrooge's personal transformation. It reminds him that his encounter with the Ghost is time-limited, and he must heed the lessons and insights the spirit has to offer in the present moment to effect meaningful change.

In conclusion, "My time grows short" is a pivotal quote in "A Christmas Carol" that underscores the urgency and impermanence of time, the significance of living in the present, and the potential for personal transformation. It serves as a catalyst for Scrooge's evolving understanding of the holiday's true meaning and the importance of embracing the spirit of Christmas in his life.

QUOTATION 30

"The chain was of cash boxes, keys, padlocks, ledgers, deeds, and heavy purses wrought in steel."

The quote, "The chain was of cash-boxes, keys, padlocks, ledgers, deeds, and heavy purses wrought in steel" is a vivid and symbolic description of Jacob Marley's ghostly chain in Charles Dickens' "A Christmas Carol." This passage serves as a powerful and haunting representation of the consequences of Marley's actions during his life, as well as a warning to Ebenezer Scrooge about his own path. Let's delve into the different layers of meaning in this quote:

1. Material Attachments: The elements of the chain, including cash boxes, keys, padlocks, ledgers, deeds, and heavy purses, are all associated with money and wealth. They symbolize the materialistic and profit-driven pursuits that consumed Marley during his lifetime. Each item on the chain represents a specific aspect of his greed and financial obsession.

2. Unbreakable Bonds: The use of "wrought in steel" emphasizes the unyielding and unbreakable nature of the chain. It reflects the permanence of the impact of one's actions and choices in life. Marley's chain of materialism has become a burden he must carry for eternity.

3. **Spiritual Consequences:** Marley's chain is not a physical burden but a spiritual one. It represents the moral and ethical debts he accumulated during his life. Each cash box, ledger, or deed represents a transaction that reflects a lack of empathy

59

and compassion for others. Marley's punishment in the afterlife is to bear the weight of his own moral failings.

4. A Warning to Scrooge: The description of Marley's chain serves as a warning to Scrooge. It foreshadows the potential fate that awaits him if he does not change his miserly and selfish ways. It implies that Scrooge's own spiritual burden, his future chain, will grow heavier if he does not embrace a more compassionate and generous approach to life.

5. The Symbol of Regret: Marley's chain becomes a symbol of his deep regret and remorse in the afterlife. He is tormented by the realization that he wasted his life pursuing wealth at the expense of human relationships and kindness.

6. A Commentary on Society: Beyond the individual characters, Marley's chain is also a commentary on the broader social and economic issues of Dickens' time. It reflects the harsh realities of economic disparities and the negative consequences of unbridled capitalism, especially on the lives of the less fortunate.

In summary, the quote, "The chain was of cash-boxes, keys, padlocks, ledgers, deeds, and heavy purses wrought in steel" is a striking visual representation of the spiritual and moral burdens individuals carry due to their actions in life. It emphasizes the corrosive effects of materialism and greed, serves as a warning to those who follow similar paths, and provides a powerful vehicle for Dickens to critique the social and economic injustices of his era. Marley's chain is a central symbol in the novella, encapsulating its themes of redemption, transformation, and the true meaning of Christmas.

.

Printed in Great Britain
by Amazon

37783484R00040